Go on the A

To begin and end this lifetime is like ocean and thinking that we know all there is to know about it because we've seen the waves and measured the tides.

Just as what we did yesterday shaped today, what we do today shapes tomorrow. When you are aware of your past life experiences, you can recall and take advantage of the strengths, knowledge and wisdom that you have acquired in other lifetimes, and use those things to help your life today. Not only do you have the potential to free yourself from the self-defeating patterns you've developed in other lifetimes—you can gain the insight you need to make your life more productive and fulfilling.

Those who accept the idea of reincarnation understand why death is like summer vacation between school terms. Eternal life is not something you'll achieve in some misty future—*you already possess it. The Truth About Past Life Regression* will help you claim your full birthright as an unlimited spirit!

About the Author

Florence Wagner McClain has spent almost 30 years in the study of the mind and experimenting with man's mental potentials, hypnosis, memory enhancement, the various psychic sciences and metaphysics. She has spent over ten years teaching and lecturing in the fields of mental and psychic development. She has participated in 2,000 past-life regressions, which is comparable to or in excess of the experiences of anyone working in that field.

To Write to the Author

If you wish to contact the author or would like more information about this book, please write to the author in care of Llewellyn Worldwide, and we will forward your request. Both the author and publisher appreciate hearing from you and learning of your enjoyment of this book and how it has helped you. Llewellyn Worldwide cannot guarantee that every letter written to the author can be answered, but all will be forwarded. Please write to:

Florence Wagner McClain
c/o Llewellyn Worldwide
P.O. Box 64383-359, St. Paul, MN 55164-0383, U.S.A.

Please enclose a self-addressed, stamped envelope for reply, or $1.00 to cover costs.
If outside U.S.A., enclose international postal reply coupon.

Free Catalog from Llewellyn

For more than 90 years Llewellyn has brought its readers knowledge in the fields of metaphysics and human potential. Learn about the newest books in spiritual guidance, natural healing, astrology, occult philosophy and more. Enjoy book reviews, new age articles, a calendar of events, plus current advertised products and services. To get your free copy of *Llewellyn's New Worlds of Mind and Spirit*, send your name and address to:

Llewellyn's New Worlds
P.O. Box 64383-359, St. Paul, MN 55164-0383, U.S.A.

LLEWELLYN'S VANGUARD SERIES

The Truth About

PAST LIFE REGRESSION

by Florence Wagner McClain

1994
Llewellyn Publications
St. Paul, MN 55164-0383, U.S.A.

FIRST EDITION, 1986
Second Edition
First Printing, 1994

International Standard Book Number:
0-87542-359-0

LLEWELLYN PUBLICATIONS
A Division of Llewellyn Worldwide, Ltd.
P.O. Box 64383, St. Paul, MN 55164-0383

Other Books by Florence Wagner McClain

A Practical Guide to Past Life Regression

Llewellyn Publications is the oldest publisher of New Age Sciences in the Western Hemisphere. This book is one of a series of introductory explorations of each one of the many fascinating dimensions of New Age Science—each important to a new understanding of Body and Soul, Mind and Spirit, of Nature and humanity's place in the world, and the vast unexplored regions of Microcosm and Macrocosm.

Please write for a full lost of publications.

INTRODUCTION

Have we really lived in other physical bodies in other times and places? The only person who can answer that question is you, by the individual, personal experience of remembering your own past lives through regression.

Past life regression is safe and simple. The overly dramatized episodes seen on television or in the movies have almost nothing in common with the real experience. It can be a valuable tool for gaining insight into yourself and solving problems. And—it can also open the door to adventure.

LOST TREASURE

"Turn here? What do you mean, turn here? That's a dead end. I don't know why I let you talk me into this."

"Please, Greg, just a little longer. I know we're almost there."

Greg turned the car into the short dirt lane and stopped as the ruts ended at a barbed wire fence. Sandy was immediately out of the car and through the fence and halfway across the meadow by the time Greg grudgingly followed.

"I can't believe that you are doing this. I can't believe that I've driven a hundred miles on this wild goose chase because of some stupid parlor game. Most of all, I can't believe that you really think you remembered a past life."

"It isn't a wild goose chase, and you'll just have to experience regression for yourself to understand."

"I understand that I'm going back to the car and wait until you have come to your senses."

"Wait. Look. There is the creek just like I remembered. Come on. It's only about a quarter of a mile now."

Greg shook his head and followed Sandy into the thick growth of pecan and oak along the creek bottom.

"There, I told you. See. I did remember."

Greg felt a prickly thrill along his spine. The scene was just as Sandy had described it. The high creek banks had been worn into a deep cut which was obviously a crossing, and the deep ruts were still visible trailing off into brush on one side and a meadow on the other.

The young man absent-mindedly scuffed at a half-buried object and reached to pick it up as it broke free from the soft dirt. The wheel hub from a wagon—or perhaps an old stagecoach. His hand shook.

"Sandy, please start from the beginning and tell me what you remembered."

"Well, I was 13 when I held up the stagecoach here at this crossing. We were desperately poor. A grass fire had burned our crops, and we were facing a winter with little food and no money. Ma and Pa had gone to town to see if they could find work. My 14-year-old brother had gone hunting, so I was home alone.

"I dressed in some of Johnny's overalls, tucked my hair up under an old hat, and loaded Pa's pistol. I thought that if I tied a rag across my face I'd look like a man. I knew about when to expect the stagecoach. I had hidden in the under-brush and spied on it several times, wishing I could go traveling to some far-off place. I knew also that the stagecoach would have to slow almost to a stop to make this crossing.

"The coach was late that day. I had almost given up when I heard it coming. I pulled the rag over my face and stepped out here with the pistol when the stagecoach was down there in the creek bed. I yelled for the driver to stop. Then I saw the man on horseback. He had been on the far side of the coach. He came riding toward me laughing and saying he wasn't going to be held up by any kid.

"The next thing I knew the pistol in my hand fired, and the man fell off his horse. I thought I'd killed him. I panicked, jumped on the horse and galloped off toward home. A mile or so away, I sent the horse in one direction and I ran in the other. The only thing I took was a leather bag which hung from the saddle horn.

"When I got home, I changed into my dress and hid Johnny's overalls and Pa's pistol. I looked in the leather bag. There were two silver dollars and a bundle of greenbacks. I was certain that there would be a posse on my trail any minute, and they'd hang me for murder. I couldn't think of any way to explain the money, so I dug a hole under the rain barrel at the comer of the house and buried it."

"Did you ever dig it up?"

"No, but I'm going to—today."

Greg followed Sandy back to the car and drove where she directed as she continued recount-ing her past life memory.

"My parents came home full of news about the holdup, and I was relieved to find out that I'd only shot the man in the shoulder. He was quite angry, however, and had offered a reward for the return of his horse and saddlebag, and a chance to 'bust the kid that done it.'

"From the description of 'the kid,' my parents were afraid that my brother Johnny might have had something to do with the holdup. He insisted that he had been squirrel hunting, and he had the squirrel's to show for his effort. They never quite believed him. There were tumors and speculations throughout the community, and Johnny's name was mentioned more than once.

"I didn't realize how much it bothered Johnny until he died from pneumonia three years later. His last words were: 'I didn't do it. I didn't rob the stage.'

"I felt so ashamed and so guilty that I could never bring myself to tell anyone what I had done. Every time I walked outside, that rain barrel and the guilty secret under it just seemed to be sitting there ready to shout my guilt to the whole world.

"This has helped me to understand why, in this lifetime, I've always been fanatical about not even taking a paper clip that doesn't belong to me. But I've always felt guilty, like someone was about to accuse me of stealing. In the stores I always feel like everyone is looking at me and thinking that I'm shoplifting. I always feel guilty if anything is missing when I'm around. I guess I just never got over feeling guilty for what I did in that lifetime. But now that I understand, I can be free of those feelings."

By this time, Sandy and Greg had driven several miles down a farm road into the area where

Sandy felt certain she could find the place she and her family had lived. Greg stopped the car, and they walked across a meadow, down a hill, and into a small valley bisected by a dry creek bed.

"There. It should be there." Sandy pointed into the middle of a plum thicket. "Yes. There isn't much left. Just a few stones from the fireplace and chimney. Over there, see that depression? That's where the outhouse was."

Sandy looked at the remains of the fireplace and visualized the outlines of the house in her mind's eye. "Here, just about here. This is where the rain barrel sat." Sandy started digging with the small folding shovel she had brought along. The ground was hard and laced with roots, but she persisted until she had a hole about 18 inches deep.

The dirt became very discolored, and the mass of fibrous material was barely recognizable as a rotted leather bag with a rusted buckle. There was a mass which might have been a bundle of greenbacks. A little deeper in the hole were two tarnished pieces of metal half fused together—two silver dollars.

"It's true. It's really true," Sandy whispered. "And all that pain and misery, then and now, over this."

"Now look here, Sandy," Greg said sternly, "can you swear that the only knowledge you had about this came from that past life regression?"

"Absolutely, Greg. Absolutely."

Greg wandered away while Sandy sat and thought about the new perspective the regression and the experiences of the day had given her on her life. How difficult it was to believe that something as impermanent as this mass of rotted leather had caused her to waste one lifetime, and live with guilt and limitations in this one. She mentally severed the remaining emotional ties as she dropped the mass back into the hole and covered it.

"Sandy, how old was Johnny when he died?" Greg called from a nearby rise surrounded by a grove of trees. "And what was your name?"

"He was 17. My name was Sarah, Sarah Peters. Why?"

"You have to look at this."

Sandy suddenly remembered what was located on that rise. Her heart beat a little faster as she stepped into the tiny family cemetery and saw the weathered stones with the barely discernible names of her mother and father and her 17-year-old brother, and another: "Sarah—spinster daughter of Daniel and Jessie Peters."

"That's awesome, Sandy, really awesome. You say that past life regression is fairly easy?"

THOUGHTS OF IMMORTALITY

Sandy and Greg had the unusual adventure of being able to follow through on information from Sandy's past life regression and find physical evidence to support her memories. Often this is not possible, but when it does happen, the emotions are indescribable. There is almost nothing which can give one the sense of being immortal and eternal as can the experience of standing at a grave and remembering the life you lived in the body which is buried there.

It is at such moments that you understand that eternal life is not something you work toward in some far-off future time. You are already immortal. And, it is at such moments that you truly understand what an unimportant, impermanent thing death is. Death is like summer vacation between school terms.

ALCOHOLIC MEMORIES

Albert James experienced past life regression and remembered an episode which dramatically changed his whole life.

Albert was an alcoholic. He had been through various programs with a degree of success. He could keep himself from drinking most of the time, but the desire to drink was constantly with him. The effort required to stay sober kept him functioning at the outer limits of his emotional and mental resources. There was little time in his life for his family or job—he barely held on to both—because almost every waking thought was engaged in the battle not to drink.

After many frustrating years, one of Albert's friends suggested that he try past life regression therapy as a possible means of help. Albert was willing to try anything, even though he wasn't quite sure what past life regression was.

After being helped by suggestion to relax, Albert was directed to mentally return to the point in time where his drinking problem had originated. He remembered his most recent past lifetime when he had worked in construction, helping to build railroads across the American wilderness.

One day as a cut for a railroad bed was being blasted through a rocky ridge, one of the dynamite charges misfired, and Albert was caught in a rock slide. Albert was directed to remember this experience without feeling any pain or distress of any nature. He detached himself emotionally from the experience as he remembered receiving massive crushing injuries from the waist down.

The country was hot and dry. The men were always a little short of water as it had to be hauled to the work site. Not only did Albert suffer from terrible pain, but also from heat and thirst. It took almost three days for Albert to die. The only comfort and freedom from pain he had during that time was when one of the men found enough whiskey to knock him out.

Albert died with a raging thirst, and a driving desire for more whiskey.

This past life regression gave Albert a great deal of insight into himself. He remembered that even as a child in this present lifetime he had always felt thirsty and had consumed enormous quantities of liquids. The family doctor had found him to be in good health, so his mother and father had ceased to be concerned about his inordinate thirst. At the age of 19, Albert was in a motorcycle accident. One leg was severely injured and broken. Albert suddenly began to crave alcohol, and that craving had ruled his life ever since.

At the end of the regression experience, Albert was given the suggestion that because he now understood the reason for his desire for alcohol, he no longer needed to react to it. He was instructed, "You will bring with you the beneficial knowledge of why you have had the strong desire to drink alcoholic beverages. You will leave behind, on all levels of mind, the detrimental need and desire to drink alcoholic beverages. You will be in full control of your desires and responses."

After this past life regression experience, situations which triggered a desire to drink became increasingly rare. Albert found that he needed only to take a few seconds to mentally negate and release the desire. Within a few weeks, Albert lost all desire for alcohol and has not experienced a recurrence of that desire in 15 years.

IS BELIEF NECESSARY?

It is not necessary for you to believe in reincarnation to experience the benefits of past life regression. Whatever decision you make concerning the validity of reincarnation is immaterial as far as the benefits of the experience are concerned. 'Reliving' what seem to be past life experiences helps to provide answers to problems and great insight into yourself. It helps you to stand back and take a more objective look at your strengths and weaknesses, and your life goals. It gives aid in understanding and freeing yourself from fears and detrimental habits.

The past life regression experience generates a more tolerant outlook on life, and helps to put things in their proper perspective. It is difficult to maintain prejudice and bigotry when you can remember being members of other races. Death loses its mystery and threat. Past life regression is not a magic cure-all, but it is a valuable tool for enhancing the quality of your present life.

WHAT IS REINCARNATION?

Reincarnation is the theory that man's soul, or awareness, survives death, and returns at varying intervals to be born into another physical body for the purpose of growing in knowledge, wisdom and self-awareness.

Part of the belief is that we each experience life as male and female, as members of the various races and social and economic classes. It doesn't matter one little bit if you remember lifetimes as royalty or as a slave, or a lifetime as a corporation president or a janitor. We have all been there or will be. Status, wealth and social position all disappear at death. Lessons learned and growth gained from the various experiences are what remain, and we are the sum of all of our past experiences.

Great and mighty deeds don't count for any more than faithful attention to the routines of ordinary life, unless the motivations match the deeds. The motivations behind our actions and whether we learned and grew from the experiences are the important aspects.

TALENTS

You can see the reflections of your past life experiences and knowledge in your daily life. Perhaps you have a particular talent in art, music, language, or science. Chances are that you have been involved with those things in recent past lives, and are enjoying some of the benefits of past efforts. This is particularly true in the cases of child prodigies.

A young woman was interested in learning to fly. At her first lesson, the instructor was astonished as the young woman automatically took the controls of the plane and flew it with great expertise. He could not, in fact would not, believe that she had never before flown. The young woman had no explanation, other than that she just knew what to do. At a later time, a past life regression revealed that she had been a pilot during the early days of aviation.

ANXIETY EXPLAINED

On the other hand, you may experience fears for which no explanation can be found in your present lifetime. Perhaps there are unexplained frictions in certain relationships. Perhaps there are certain places or things which make you unhappy or cause distress for no reason that you can understand.

There was a man and a woman who were friends. The man seldom took a drink except on certain rare social occasions. On these occasions the woman would experience an intense anxiety attack, even though she was not physically present. Knowing that he was going to attend such a function, or his telling about it afterward, was enough to precipitate an attack.

When quizzed about her feelings, she said that the idea of him taking a drink made her feel extremely threatened and very much afraid. She always had the compulsion to beg him to promise not to take a drink. Many times she would cry and shake, and she always felt like a complete fool because of her reaction.

A subsequent past life regression revealed a recent lifetime in which the man and woman had been business partners, and extraordinarily close friends. The man had been an alcoholic, and his drinking had caused an automobile accident which had killed both of them. Once the basis for the anxiety was understood, the attacks ceased.

TRANSMIGRATION

There are many misconceptions about reincarnation, and one of the most common is that people reincarnate as animals or insects. This belief is called transmigration. Of the 75% of the world's population which believe in reincarnation, only a tiny percent believe in transmigration.

Reincarnation is the belief that the soul of man survives death and returns to be born into another physical body—a human body. Past life regression information has failed to support the theory of transmigration.

It would appear that the theory of transmigration evolved from a misunderstanding of ancient allegories and teachings intended to instruct man about his relationship with other forms of life, and his responsibility for all life forms.

The spark of life which animates the cells of our bodies comes from the same Source which gives life to all things. Therefore, we are one with all life. We should develop an attitude of respect for all life, and act in a responsible manner toward all living things.

We are spirits who must have a physical body to inhabit so that we may function in a physical world. Otherwise we are just ghosts. Our physical bodies are composed of colonies of living cells, each performing specific functions and cooperating together to provide an efficient host for our souls. Therefore, we should treat the life forms which make up our body with the care and respect they deserve.

In a similar way, we human beings are cell colonies on the planet. This planet is a living entity and is our host for our periods of reincarnation. We have a responsibility to respect, cherish, heal and renew the Earth in every way possible, because one of the functions of our 'cell colony' is meant to be as caretakers of the Earth.

CHRISTIANITY AND REINCARNATION

Christianity embraced and taught the doctrine of reincarnation until the Emperor Justinian summoned the Fifth Ecumenical Congress of Constantinople in 543 A.D. This congress was convened for the expressed purpose of censoring from the religious literature and teachings of the day all references to reincarnation.

Reincarnation was not a popular doctrine with the nobility of the day since it essentially taught that all men were equal. This made difficulties for the nobility who wanted to convince the common man of their divinity. How distressing when one considered that he might be in the beggar's place the next lifetime, and the beggar in his place.

Also, the doctrine of reincarnation made man personally responsible for himself and his spiritual development, and promoted the idea that man could find the truth for himself. This was unpopular with the church officials. The 'common man' was never encouraged to think for himself.

In spite of efforts to destroy them, there remain several references in the Bible which address the issue of reincarnation.

In Matthew 16:13, Jesus asked his disciples who people thought he was. The disciples told him that some people thought he was John the Baptist returned to life. Others thought he was Elijah or Jeremiah, or one of the other great prophets of ancient times. People evidently believed in reincarnation at that time.

Later, in Matthew 17:10-13, after Jesus had stated his claim that he was the Christ, the One who had been prophesied, the disciples questioned him. They asked why, if he was the Messiah, the prophets had said that Elijah would come again before the Messiah. Jesus told them that Elijah had been reborn, and they hadn't recognized him. Then they understood that he meant John the Baptist. *Jesus claimed that John the Baptist* was *the reincarnation of Elijah.*

John 9:1-3 presents the story of a man who had been born blind. Jesus is questioned by his disciples, "Master, who did sin, *this man* or his parents that he was born blind?" Jesus answered that neither had sinned. The man had been born blind so that the power of God could be demonstrated.

Notice that no one, including Jesus, seemed to find anything absurd in the idea that the blind man could have performed some act before his birth to have caused his blindness at birth.

RESPONSIBILITY FOR ACTIONS

Those who do not understand the theory of reincarnation often assume that those who believe are attracted to the idea because it frees a person from responsibility for his actions. "You can just do whatever you want to in this lifetime and not be concerned, because you can come back and have another chance."

Actually, one of the main lessons taught by reincarnation is that of personal responsibility. The more one investigates and understands the mechanics of reincarnation, the more aware one becomes of the consequences of each thought and action. When you begin to recognize the role which past actions have played in creating both the desirable and the undesirable elements of your present life, this becomes a very strong motivation to make every effort to be the best you can be today, to build a better tomorrow.

PURPOSE OF REINCARNATION

The purpose of reincarnation is to provide opportunities for you to come to a knowledge of your true nature. You are an evolving, unlimited spirit created by and in the image of the Ultimate, Unlimited Spirit. As you accept full responsibility for your thoughts and actions, and free yourself from the limitations of the physical existence, then you no longer need the lessons which are to be learned in a physical world. You have no need to continue in the cycles of death and rebirth. You have earned your right to claim your full birthright as unlimited spirit.

DOCUMENTED REINCARNATION

One of the most intriguing documented examples of reincarnation is that of the present Dalai Lama. This Buddhist leader, exiled from his homeland of Tibet, is known as the Fourteenth Incarnation of the Dalai Lama.

Shortly before the thirteenth Dalai Lama died, he prophesied to certain trusted emissaries circumstances which would surround his rebirth. About three years after the Dalai Lama's death, the acting regent had a vision in which he saw a certain house where a child had been born as the reincarnation of the Dalai Lama. Much later, when the appropriate time had come, the regent quietly set out with search parties to find the place and the child. Eventually, the secret search led them out of Tibet and across the border into China. There, the house which the regent had seen in his vision was found. The servants and the lamas exchanged clothing. This gave the lamas the freedom to visit the kitchens and areas where the children might be found.

A four-year-old boy met the disguised lamas and correctly identified them and where they had come from. He also asked for the necklace the regent was wearing, saying that it had belonged to him (the child) when he was the Thirteenth Incarnation of the Dalai Lama. This was true.

The circumstances of his birth fulfilled the prophesies he had made. He also had certain physical characteristics which had been foretold. Later, he correctly identified his personal possessions from among many similar items, and successfully passed many stringent spiritual and physical tests which confirmed him as the Fourteenth Incarnation of the Dalai Lama.

THEATER EARTH

Earth is similar to a theater in which there is a continuously running drama. We make our appearance upon the Earth to play a chosen role, and when that role is finished we leave to prepare ourselves for the next role.

With each role we put on the costume of the body we have chosen—male or female, attractive or unattractive—of whatever race we have picked. But, whatever costume we choose to wear to play our chosen roles, it is still *you* or *me*, souls, in appropriate disguise for our current debut at Theater Earth.

The soul is neither male or female. The soul has no race. The soul is spirit, that part of us which is immortal, that part of us which is aware that we exist.

WRITING OUR ROLES

It would appear that we write our own roles, or draw up a type of blueprint for each lifetime. Most individuals never get a look at the script or blueprint after the present life begins. Using past life regression, it is possible to review the blueprint which you created for your present lifetime.

You did ask to be born. Not only that, you chose the time, the place, the circumstances and the people. And you probably chose those particular conditions for just exactly the reasons you are presently telling yourself you wouldn't. But you didn't choose the situations to be easy or idyllic. You chose them to develop strength in areas where you were weak, to learn patience and tolerance, to learn compassion, to learn self-reliance, to gain a sense of your self-worth, to learn to love and to learn to let go, and to learn the limits of your personal responsibilities—all that and much more.

Through past life regression you can learn how to look at that blueprint, and perhaps understand and get rid of some of the frustrations in your life. It can provide for you the opportunity to gain the insight you need to decide what the appropriate courses of action are to make your life more productive and fulfilling.

WHAT IS PAST LIFE REGRESSION?

Past life regression is just remembering. Stored in your subconscious mind are the memories of all of your experiences since you became a soul with the awareness of your individuality. Regression is reaching into those memory banks to recapture the events of past lifetimes. It isn't so very different from trying to remember events which took place during your early childhood. At first the memories may be dim and few, but each event remembered sparks another memory and another until it becomes easy.

In one way you might compare it to an information storage system which has had little or no use for a long period of time. Some of the file drawers are stuck, or rusty. There are a few cobwebs here and there. Dust is thick and fills the air making it difficult to see. Some of the lightbulbs have burned out, and the file clerk has taken an extended vacation.

But—a little attention here and there, putting the system on notice that you intend to make extensive use of it, and everything slowly begins to shift into gear. Shortly the system is running efficiently, retrieving the memories and information you request.

There are many ways to get the attention of your 'file clerk,' or gain access to your subconscious. Nearly everyone has experienced a form of spontaneous regression. For example, have you ever met someone for the first time, but felt an immediate kinship as if you were old and intimate friends? You probably were friends in some past lifetime, and the presence of that soul caused your subconscious to produce the proper emotion for that far-past relationship.

Perhaps you have traveled to some strange place only to find that it is familiar to you—you have a feeling of being at home. No doubt it was home to you sometime in the past. These are not uncommon experiences.

Very young children often have fairly clear memories of past lives. Sometimes these memories take the form of daydreams or are acted out in play. Occasionally past life memories are the basis for some of the fears of childhood. The child who is afraid of water may have memories of having drowned in another lifetime. The child who is afraid of the dark or can't bear to be in a confined area may have, at least, the emotional memories of the POW who was kept in the dark or confined in a small cage. Children usually forget their past life memories rather quickly as they approach school age.

Some individuals have gained a certain amount of access to their subconscious through the practice of meditation. Probably the most familiar method of gaining access to the subconscious is through conventional hypnosis under the guidance of a trained hypnotherapist. Possibly the easiest and quickest way to gain access to the subconscious is through guided relaxation. Simple instructions are available in a recent book on past life regression. You can be guided by a friend, and later you can guide yourself, through exercises which will give you access to your subconscious and past life memories on demand. Using this method, you remain alert and aware and in complete control of yourself and the experience.

WHY REMEMBER?

Every spiritual philosophy and every psychological discipline, in one way or another, conveys the directive of "Know thyself." To begin and end the knowing of ourselves with this present lifetime is equivalent to looking at the surface of the ocean and thinking that we know all there is to know about it because we have seen the waves and measured the tide.

You are the sum of all of your past experiences. The more you can remember of your past life experiences, the more you can understand and be in control of how these experiences affect your relationships with others and your reactions to the world around you. The more you are in control of your life, the freer you are.

When you are aware of your past life experiences, you can recall and take advantage of the strengths, the knowledge, and the wisdom which you have acquired in other lifetimes and use those things to help you in your daily life. You can become aware of any negative or self-defeating patterns which you have developed in other lifetimes, and change those habits or attitudes so that you do not continue the detrimental cycles.

In one situation, a young man repeatedly found himself about to reach goals he had set for himself, but each time he would seem to make a deliberate decision to do something which would ensure his failure. A past life regression revealed that he had worked very hard to be a successful businessman in a past life and had succeeded. He had acquired great wealth and power, but it had changed the attitudes of his friends and family toward him, and he ended up alone and very unhappy. This had caused a deep-seated fear in this present lifetime that if he succeeded in achieving his goals he would be unhappy and alone. He was able to release this fear and understand that success did not mean unhappiness. He has achieved his first set of goals and is making rapid progress toward the next set.

Have you struggled with frustrations and fears which seem to have no basis in your present life? Have you tried your best to build good relationships with certain people but it just never quite works out? Has everyone given you reams of advice which never quite fit your particular situation? No matter how hard you try, do things never quite click into place?

Using past life regression, you can make your own investigations and find your own answers.

Venturing into your own subconscious and retrieving past life memories can provide high adventure, as well as unusual insight. And, it can free you from the fear of death.

MAN'S NEED TO KNOW

As long as we live in a world where neighbor hates neighbor because of skin color or political or religious affiliations, and solves its problems with violence or escape into drugs, alcohol, or casual sex, we're all losers. Something is dreadfully wrong when one human being is considered less than another because of being male or female, when thousands of young lives are lost every year to suicide, and when one's worth as a human being is measured by material wealth or social status. It is tragic when a person who spends his or her life happily married to the same person is considered an oddity. It is tragic when we or our brothers feel alone and without purpose in the Universe. We all lose when any man refuses to take responsibility for his actions, or lives or dies in fear.

When man understands that the material wealth and power he gives his all to acquire today won't count for anything in tomorrow's world, he will do all in his power to build riches of character, wisdom, knowledge and soul-bonds with friends and family which will enrich his existence forever.

Through past life regression, through remembering his own creation, man will find that the emptiness he feels can be filled with a knowledge of his true nature and his rightful place in the Universe. As he strives to know himself, he will begin to know the Unlimited Spirit of which he is a part. Then man will know that he is never alone, never without hope, and never without purpose to his existence. This is why man needs to remember.

WHAT IS KARMA?

Karma is the law of cause and effect. Simply that, and nothing more. Of all the misunderstood and abused aspects of reincarnation, karma heads the list. When something unpleasant happens, it is very common to see people who don't even believe in reincarnation shrug their shoulders and hear them say, "Must be my karma." This is unfortunate because it perpetuates the idea that anything bad or unpleasant is karma, and gives a distorted idea of what karma is. If you want a definition of karma in Biblical terms, karma is reaping what you sow. Or, you might define karma as the meeting of self.

For every action there is a reaction. This is a Universal law, and is unchanging and beyond our control. What is within our control is the action we do or the cause we set into motion, and the attitudes with which we deal with the reactions or effects.

Since karma is neither good nor bad, then it is the applications we make of it which makes it into a negative or positive influence in our lives. Karma was never intended as a system of rewards and punishments. The intent of the law of karma is to teach us that we are personally responsible for our lives, and to help us learn to live in harmony with the Universe.

Through the use of past life regression, it is possible to gain an overall view of the various causes or cycles that we have set into motion in other lifetimes which are continuing to have an effect on this present life. This is like opening the doors of a treasure vault. Laid out in front of you is one of the greatest treasures man can have— knowledge. You can see the error in judgement you have made, and the results of those errors. You can see how to take advantage of the situation, turn it into something beneficial, and avoid repetition of those mistakes.

THE TREASURE CHESTS OF RECOVERED KNOWLEDGE

In those treasure chests of your far memory is all the knowledge you have acquired in all your many lifetimes. That knowledge can be reviewed and retrieved. In other treasure chests of your mind there are the skills and talents you have developed in other lifetimes. Those skills and talents are there for you to remember and use if you choose.

In still other niches of your mind may be the emotional records of traumatic events which may have happened in other lifetimes. These events may hold the answers to that terrible fear you have of fire, heights, snakes, or the dark. The fact that you starved to death in another lifetime may just be the last piece of information you need to get in control of that weight problem. Being able to remember the events which are at the roots of such problems, one can understand, release the trauma or influence, and no longer be affected by it.

Part of our responsibility in dealing with our karma is to make certain that we are not allowing ourselves to be controlled by such past events. Also, through past life regression we can determine whether we have exercised our free will in the wisest manner in choosing how to deal with our karma.

If a person still believes that karma is meant as a system of punishment and reward, he or she may have chosen a hard and unnecessary pathway for himself or herself. For instance, if he or she caused some-one to suffer mentally or physically in a past life, he or she may have chosen a life filled with suffering as a means to atone. To deliberately generate more suffering and misery in the world does not atone, and does not benefit anyone. If, however, through a desire to make up for suffering caused in other lifetimes, he or she turns his or her efforts to the alleviation of suffering, this brings positive benefits for all concerned.

Perhaps the saddest misunderstanding and misuse of karma is the person who uses it as an excuse to avoid helping others. More people than one might suppose use a distorted idea of karma to avoid personal responsibility. "Oh, I wouldn't dream of helping that person. It may be his karma to be . . . (sick, hurt, hungry, in danger, etc.). I wouldn't want to overrule God's will." This presupposes several things, and expresses much arrogance. First, it suggests that it is "God's Will" that people be miserable in some way. Then there is the arrogant assumption that if it was God's will, they could overrule it. That doesn't say much for some people's opinion of a Supreme Being. But—if you want to suppose all the above, then how do you know that it isn't your karma to help that person? None of that philosophy fits into the balanced, logical framework of reincarnation and karma.

WHAT TO EXPECT IN REGRESSION

If you are experiencing a past life regression through the means of guided relaxation, you can initially expect to feel deeply relaxed and peaceful. As you are guided into a past life, you will be mentally alert and aware of where you are and what you are doing. You will be in control so that you may stop or control the direction of the regression at any point.

You will receive the information from your subconscious in one or more ways. No one way is any more accurate or any better than another. As you are asked questions to awaken the memories, you may feel as if you are reliving the lifetime with all of the sensory input. You will, however, be instructed not to experience any pain or distress. The most common experience is to receive the memories as if you were watching television or a movie. You are detached, but watching the lifetime unfold on your mental screen.

Some people simply 'know' the answers to the questions they are asked and have little or no visual impressions. Others feel or hear or obtain information in a combination of ways. At first, information received may be sketchy, but as you gain a little experience, the memories will be clearer and easier to retrieve. You will find that after experiencing regression, you will have spontaneous memories of other lifetimes.

LIFE AFTER DEATH

Your level of experience and your desire will determine how to explore a past life regression. You may relive your death, explore the period after death and your activities until you choose to be reborn. Experiencing death in this manner is not traumatic, because it is done in a detached manner. The period directly after death often proves to be somewhat humorous, since the person usually stays around for a few days to observe his funeral and the immediate reactions to his death, and often has some interesting comments to make.

It would appear that after death there is a period of rest, then a self-evaluation and the beginning of a blueprint for the next lifetime. During the period of planning there seems to be individual and group class type of situations. There may be only a short time between lifetimes, or several centuries may pass.

At first introduction to reincarnation, the idea of returning to live again and again may seem exciting and inviting, especially to someone who is afraid of death. As more is understood and experienced through regression, personal attitudes change into a desire to learn and grow as quickly as possible, so that one doesn't have to come back again.

After experiencing your own death in several different lifetimes, you lose the fear of death. It becomes no more than just another part of the cycle—a birth from the physical world into the non-physical world.

If you stop and think about it, in one way or another, we expend a lot of time and energy being afraid of death—not in working to be healthy and prolong our lives, but just in being afraid of death, the Great Unknown. When the unknown is known and the fear no longer there, that time and energy can be turned to living.

Finally, at the conclusion of a past life regression, positive statements are made releasing any negative or detrimental influences from past lives, and reinforcing the positive and beneficial influences. An individual ends a regression feeling rested and relaxed. Functioning at those particular levels of mind is refreshing and revitalizing.

MEMORIES

After exploring several lifetimes through past life regression, it may appear that the other lifetimes were much more dramatic and exciting than the present one. That is just how memories work. We don't usually remember the dull or ordinary days.

It seems as if a majority of the time when the subject of reincarnation or regression is discussed, one would think that the world had never been populated by anything but priests and priestesses, kings, queens, assorted nobility, Indian chiefs or the chief's daughters. Man's ego being what it is, it is much more appealing to be a leader than a follower.

Social status gained in a past lifetime is important only to the immature ego. What you did, how much you learned and whether you matured and grew from the experience is much more important than whether you did it as a member of high society, as 'just a housewife,' as a multi-millionaire tycoon, or as a poor dirt farmer. What you are is what lasts from lifetime to—who you were.

UNEXPECTED BENEFITS

Judith was feeling increasingly frustrated. She wanted to do something creative, but had no talent that she was aware of. She thought about taking some type of class—perhaps art—but that didn't really appeal to her. During a past life regression, she discovered a lifetime during which she had made jewelry and had been a skilled needle-woman, making embroidered wall hangings.

Judith was delighted. She made a thorough exploration of the memories of that lifetime to recapture those creative skills. Soon she was designing and making occasional pieces of jewelry with a degree of skill which she, her family and friends found amazing. Even more amazing, this young woman who had seldom even sewn on a button found that she knew complicated and unusual embroidery techniques and began to turn out beautiful, intricate decorative pieces.

A LIFE SAVED

Ken, David, Erica and Mary were on an extended backpacking trip in a remote wilderness area. They were between two and three days walk from the nearest contact with civilization. Ken ignored a recurring little pain that turned out to be a small splinter which had gotten into his sock and was working its way into the instep of his foot.

That evening in camp, Ken discovered the splinter and thought he removed all of it. He ignored the apparently minor irritation. The following day was a long, hard, hot day and Ken didn't feel too well, but neither did anyone else. However, by the end of the day it was evident that while the others were just hot and tired, Ken was seriously ill and feverish. When he removed his boot, his foot was badly inflamed and infected, and an angry red streak extended past his ankle. That was a good indication that Ken probably had blood poisoning. He was getting sicker by the moment. It was obvious that he couldn't walk out, and it didn't look like he would last long enough for one of the others to walk out and bring help.

Erica had experienced past life regression numerous times. She had remembered several lifetimes when she had practiced medicine—usually with an extensive knowledge of medicinal herbs. Calling on everything she could remember from those regressions, Erica opened and cleansed the wound, and applied suction using a small glass bottle partially filled with hot water. Then Erica packed the wound with a poultice prepared from garlic and certain medicinal plants she found growing in the surrounding area. She also fed Ken small amounts of garlic throughout the night. She remembered having used garlic for healing many times in past lives, and knew also that recent research had shown it to have an antibiotic effect.

By the following morning, Ken was feeling better and the infection in his foot was radically improved. Treatment was continued, and by the third morning Ken was free of fever and there was only minimal redness around the wound. Ken was able to finish the hike in fine shape.

FEARFUL UPS AND DOWNS

Walter was a sales representative for a large company. He was extremely handicapped by the fact that he was terrified of elevators. He even had difficulty riding escalators and dealing with anything which involved rapid up and down moves, such as alpine skiing or traveling in a car over hilly or mountainous roads.

This caused an unending series of problems for Walter. When possible, he would climb numerous flights of stairs to avoid an elevator. If he could not avoid use of an elevator, he would dose himself heavily with tranquilizers and then not be alert for his business meetings.

Walter had tried several approaches to solving the problem, but there always seemed to be something which eluded him about the fear and kept the treatments from being really effective. About the best he had achieved was one untranquilized elevator ride when he didn't go into complete trauma and scream or throw up.

Walter overheard two strangers in a coffee shop discussing how one of them had overcome a disabling fear of fire through past life regression. He didn't know exactly what past life regression was, but he was ready to try anything. He interrupted the conversation, and briefly explained his problem. He was given the name and phone number of someone to arrange a regression for him.

Walter was regressed back to a lifetime in which he was an out-of-work mining engineer spending his time prospecting.

He and his partner had found an old commercial operation which had been abandoned many years earlier. There was a large amount of rusting machinery. Walter and his partner had been exploring the old shafts by means of an ore bucket and a winch powered by their pack mules. One afternoon Walter had been down and was coming up in the ore bucket. He was almost to the surface when something went wrong. The ore bucket broke loose, and plummeted to the bottom of the shaft carrying Walter with it. He survived the impact by only a couple of minutes.

"That feeling," Walter said. "Oh, how I know that awful sickening feeling of having the bottom drop out from under me. That is what I have felt or anticipated every time I have gotten on an elevator, and to some degree an escalator. The best I can describe it is to tell you to remember the feeling that happens to your stomach when you hit a dip or sudden steep drop in your car. You get that funny lurch in your stomach and a thrill of fear between your shoulder blades. Well, magnify that about a hundred times, and add to it the certainty that you are about to die, and you'll understand what I have felt all these years."

Walter was given positive suggestions at the end of the regression relieving him of the negative emotional, physical, and psychological responses to the events of that past lifetime. (Often just understanding what has caused the phobia is enough to eliminate it, but positive statements made at deeper levels of mind are a good reinforcement.) Walter felt a little nervous the first couple of times he rode an elevator, but within a short while he was using elevators without a second thought.

One additional interesting note: during the past life regression Walter discovered that his partner had found a rich pocket of ore. Being greedy, he had cut the ore bucket loose with the intention of killing Walter. Walter recognized his old partner as a respected businessman in the town where he lived. "Funny," Walter commented, "everyone in town likes him and thinks he is just about perfect. I've always felt kind of strange because I felt like he was a dishonest bastard, and I have been afraid to do business with him or even turn my back on him. Maybe I can be objective now, and find out what he is really like in this lifetime."

Walter's experience brings up another point to be considered as far as karma and free will are concerned. Sometimes we are affected by decisions and actions of others which are beyond our control. How we deal with those situations is up to us. We can fret and fuss, we can turn it to our advantage, or we can do something constructive to change the situation.

A middle-aged lady with grown children tells this story of one of the most special episodes in her childhood. During WWII, when she was about 5, she and her family were moving. They were driving across a desolate area of the Southwest when a tire blew out. Tires were rationed, and it was extremely difficult to get good ones. They were about 50 miles from the nearest town. The father had to leave them (wife, daughter and 12-year-old son) and hitchhike into town to see if he could find a tire. They had very little water and food. It was hot, and the only shade came from a few scraggly bushes. All of the components for a really miserable day were there. The mother allowed the boy to use some of his scouting knowledge to look for water. She used a careful system of checks to make certain he didn't get lost, but still allowed him the adventure of roaming the wild country alone. He was eventually successful in his search for water. Presenting his full canteen, he felt ten feet tall and brother to every famous mountainman of old. Meanwhile, the mother and little girl had spread a blanket under the bushes, and had begun making an elaborate farm in the dust. Fields were fenced with tiny sticks and pebbles and plowed with fingers. Tiny green plants were placed in the rows. Houses and barns were built from stones and tiny 'logs.' Some of the water was used for a little lake. Bugs and ants were used for cattle.

It was a lovely, magical day when it could easily have been a miserable experience. More than 40 years later, those two children remember that day as one of the very special times of their childhood. It is easy to visualize a completely different day: everyone hot, miserable, complaining about the discomfort and inconvenience, children nagging the mother, mother angry and distraught. But this young mother made the decision to have a wonderful adventure, and created more than she ever dreamed.

We always have the choice as to how we deal with the situations which arise in our lives, whether those situations are the result of our own actions, or the result of other people's actions. We always have the choice as to how we deal with the karmic aspects of our lives. We can flow with the tide and usually not be pleased with the results, or we can make the decision to use every situation as a learning experience, to turn it into a positive constructive time.

AGE REGRESSION

Regression has another application which is important and useful. This is called age regression. Age regression takes one back through the present lifetime to discover answers to problems. Though it may appear that most problems have their roots in past lives, the fact is that the majority of problems are caused by events which happened in the early years of the present lifetime.

The minds of children from birth to early teens, particularly during the preschool years, are very susceptible to programming. During those years the brain operates on the same dominant frequencies which are achieved during conventional hypnosis. Therefore, a child's mind is extremely open and vulnerable to suggestion. It will accept as fact, without using any logic or reason, any information presented, particularly that which is repeated several times. Recent research even indicates that a baby's mind is affected by music, voices and other outside sounds and conditions during the last few months of pregnancy.

Many of the problems involving poor self-image and lack of a sense of self-worth can be traced to happenings during those sensitive ages. Things as varied as health problems, some learning problems, eating disorders, failure patterns, phobias and behavior problems can be the result of thoughtless words and actions directed toward young children. Likewise, success, positive attitudes and self-confidence can be the result of positive attitudes expressed to young children.

If a child is repeatedly told that he is dumb or stupid or can't learn, or can't do anything right, then he may have the mind of a genius but function well below average. On the other side, if a child is constantly reinforced with statements that he can accomplish anything he sets out to do, that he can learn anything he wants to, then there is every chance that he will be self-confidently successful.

Often, it is easy to see the evidence of negative childhood programming in adults. *You'll never amount to anything. You'll never be a man. No one will ever want you. No one can ever love someone Like you. You're fat and ugly. You're skinny and ugly. You're clumsy.* You see the results of such statements in the men who are so concerned with proving their manhood, and in the women whose sense of self-worth revolves around an appearance which never meets their standards, people who never feel that anything they do is worthwhile, and who can't accept that they are liked or loved.

Sometimes unusual or bizarre behavior patterns are set up in those early years. One woman told of the strange behavior pattern which haunted her life daily for 40 years. As far back as she could remember, she would do anything to keep from urinating. She would wait until she couldn't wait any longer, then she would either go to the bathroom, or, if she had waited too long, wet her pants. As a child when traveling, when the family would stop at a service station, she could be in agony to go to the restroom, but would deny it and refuse to go. She didn't know why she refused, and she didn't want to refuse. She often wet her pants and was humiliated by it. She wet the bed until she was a teenager, and this was a constant source of embarrassment. Her older brother teased her about this all of her life, and that didn't help her frustration. She didn't want to be the way she was, but she couldn't seem to do much about it. Her parents either ignored it, or acted as if it was some kind of willful stubbornness. Her brother continued to ridicule her. She was too embarrassed to talk to anyone about it. She finally became fairly adept at hiding her problem, but it was always there waiting to pop up at the most inopportune moment.

Finally, as a young adult she decided that something had to change. She forced herself to go to the restroom at the first feeling of need. It was a tremendously difficult battle. She had strong feelings which were a mixture of fear, guilt (as if she was doing something wrong), and relief. She also felt a great deal of defensiveness and hostility toward her mother and her brother. She could understand the feelings she had toward her brother, but it was difficult for her to understand or admit the feelings she had toward her mother.

Many years passed. The problem still lurked in the background, but seldom caused any real difficulty. The woman became involved in past life regression experiences, and eventually in age regression. She was looking for other information when she found herself at 18 months of age being seated on a potty, told that it was time to 'wee-wee,' and then slapped painfully on the leg. She didn't fully understand what she remembered until she asked her mother about it. "Oh, that was how I potty trained you. It was no trouble at all. I would put you on the potty about every two hours and slap you on the leg to make you cry. When you cried you'd relax and 'wee-wee.' I always did that whenever we were getting ready to go somewhere when you were older, too, so that you would go to the bathroom before we left the house."

This is almost a classic case of aversion therapy, and negative programming. It was extremely effective, since the punishment associated with going to the bathroom was regularly reinforced several times a day over a period of several weeks, then periodically reinforced over several years whenever the mother wanted her to go to the bathroom before they left home. Only programming which was so strongly entrenched could be that effective for so many years in disrupting a natural body function. The confusing message of "Do what I tell you to do and you will get punished," couldn't help but generate tremendous mental conflict.

Logically, the woman knew that her mother had not meant to harm her, and had not understood what she was doing, but years of misery, humiliation and anger flooded to the surface. It was difficult for her to handle it in a positive way. In another age regression she was given instructions that she no longer needed to react to that unfortunate programming, and that she would release and get rid of all emotional reactions in a positive and constructive manner. She is now freed from that early programming, and the anger.

HEALTH PROGRAMMING

Health is an area often affected by early programming. Children are repeatedly told that if they get their feet wet or get chilled, they will catch cold. There is no scientific basis for this. Colds are caused by a virus. However, on any day across the world, there are mothers and grandmothers saying, "I told you so" to little Johnny or Susie. Why? If the subconscious is subjected to repetitious information, even though the information is false, it will accept the information as true and act on it. Therefore, when a child (or even an adult under the proper circumstances relaxed in front of the TV, and "It's the flu season") is told repeatedly that a certain action or condition will produce a cold, a headache, the flu or some other physical ailment, the subconscious accepts that information as true, and sets about to trigger the body mechanisms to produce the symptoms of the expected condition. Conversely, good health and good resistance to illness can be fostered by positive statements and attitudes.

Another subtle aspect of health is often affected by early programming. Children are sometimes ignored, or only paid cursory attention by busy parents. At best, almost every parent feels that he or she really should spend more time with their children. This sets the scene for the creation of a potentially negative pattern. Little Susie or Johnny gets sick. Parents feel guilty. They surround little Susie or Johnny with loving attention, give them special presents and make them the center of their world for a little while. Susie or Johnny has the attention, and evidence of love and concern he or she craves. Then Susie or Johnny recovers, and life gradually or abruptly reverts to normal. The next time an illness or injury occurs, the sequence is repeated. It doesn't take the subconscious, or even the conscious mind, many repetitions to make the connection between being sick or injured and receiving the desired love and attention.

By the time the child grows into an adult, the negative habit pattern can be firmly entrenched in the personality. The adult produces pretend-illnesses, or dramatizes minor ones in an attempt to gain attention or keep someone's love. This may work at first, but it soon gets old and drives even friends away. Then the individual constructs more and more dramatic situations in an effort to reattract and hold the attention of the people who are drifting away. There is usually a pattern of better health between friendships or relationships, and then the pattern repeats. Sometimes the pretend-illnesses become real. This negative pattern can be corrected with age regression by taking the individual back to the particular childhood incidents and correcting the impressions he or she received which setup the negative pattern.

This situation can be prevented by never rewarding a child for being ill. Illness should be treated in a matter-of-fact manner, with only the necessary amount of attention. The child should be given attention and 'rewarded' when he is well, happy and well-behaved. This reinforces positive behavior patterns, and can make the difference between an adult who feels good to be around, or one who brings people down just by being present.

THE MIND OF MAN

The mind of man is a marvelous and complicated creation, possibly the least understood facet of the non-physical side of man. The mind is the non-physical counterpart of the brain. It resembles but exceeds the finest computer assembled by man, in that it has infinite capacity for efficient information storage and retrieval if programmed properly. The mind, however, has free will, creativity and feels emotion, things which immediately separate it from being just a computer. The scope of the mind is unlimited, and can travel through time and space in a split second. The mind can penetrate any barrier, and its memory banks survive the death of the physical body. The mind is immortal, and has the power of imagination. Nothing has ever been created which was not first created in the mind through imagination.

There are certain levels of the mind, what we call the subconscious, which manifest in brain wave activity labeled alpha, theta and delta, which are infinitely powerful for constructive or destructive purposes. These levels of mind lack the ability to reason, make value judgements, or use logic. They blindly act on whatever instruction or information is presented. Logic, reason and judgement are functions of the conscious mind or beta level. For man to be a whole being, living in the manner he was intended, he must learn to tear down the artificial barriers which have been erected between the conscious and the subconscious mind, and integrate the abilities which open the doorway into a world of infinite possibility.

If man learns to function as a whole being, then the logic or reason factor will automatically evaluate the information being fed into the subconscious and interpret it in the proper manner. He can get on with living freely in the manner he was intended, rather than having to spend time and energy dealing with the effects of randomly stored misinformation and illogical instructions which produce situations never intended. Past life regression is one way to begin to tear down that barrier.

PAST LIFE OR IMAGINATION?

Are the experiences people relive during past life regression really memories of past lives, or simply the result of an active imagination? Does it matter? Not really. Whether memory or imagination, the source of the information does not affect the validity of the experience as a problem-solving exercise.

People want to solve problems, therefore the mind wants to solve problems, and will make every effort to do so when given the opportunity. If Albert James, the alcoholic, didn't really live a lifetime as a railroad construction worker and die in an accident, does it matter? Does it matter if it was nothing more than the exercise of his imagination? The information produced allowed him to gain control of his problem.

Is Ken any less alive if Erica's medical and herbal knowledge was not remembered from past lifetimes? But, if that information did not come from past lifetimes, where did Erica's mind venture to retrieve such knowledge? That suggests some intriguing possibilities if you choose to reject the past life memory thesis. Can the mind just instantly reach out and acquire knowledge and skills it has never learned? Whatever the answer may be, past life regression is a method for personal investigation.

SOME POSSIBILITIES

Those who discount reincarnation offer various explanations for the problem-solving aspects of the information obtained. Some explain that if a situation in the present lifetime is particularly painful, distressing or embarrassing, the person involved may find it easier to deal with it by becoming detached in the guise of a past life.

It sometimes happens that a person is too emotionally involved in a problem or a relationship to objectively look at possible solutions to those problems. Or, maybe the individual is not quite emotionally mature enough to see, accept and acknowledge his or her portion of the responsibility for the situation. Could the seeming past life memories be the mind's way of injecting some objectivity into the situation, and creating a more comfortable way of acknowledging personal responsibility? The only person who can answer these questions is you, by your own experiences with past life regression.

The regression experience helps one accept personal responsibility, and aids in releasing unnecessary and unhealthy burdens of guilt. Personal relationships benefit. The insight one gains into one's own nature and potential is deeply fulfilling and comforting. Regression provides a healthy outlet and release for anger, frustration, and stress. Attitudes change. One's perspective on what is and what isn't important in life undergoes modification. People usually take a much more relaxed approach to life, and therefore become mentally, emotionally and physically healthier.

Past life regression offers a very solid potential for use in exploring, understanding and eliminating underlying causes for drug and alcohol dependency in many people. Perhaps the day will come when past life regression and age regression will be respected and valued tools for working with individuals with those problems.

The use of past life regression offers an interesting potential for the possibility of understanding and eliminating many of the ills which plague our society. If regression was accepted as a standard exercise in the development of young people, many potential problems could be understood and eliminated. The potentially violent individual could be recognized and defused. The potential addict or alcoholic could be recognized and helped before the problem surfaced. Past life influences on eating disorders, health problems, learning problems, etc., could be uncovered and resolved before they warped years of the person's life.

Positive and beneficial traits and habit patterns could be recognized and reinforced. Talents and knowledge which could aid in planned occupations in the present lifetime could be sought out, and retrieved.

Through past life regression, mankind might understand that one has a personally urgent stake in the responsible progress of technology. "Keeping the world safe and a decent place to live for our children and grandchildren" is an ambitious statement which is often heard, but rarely carries any weight when decisions are made in the worlds of business and science. Bad and irresponsible decisions are often made because they are expedient and profitable, and the individuals involved have a self-centered point of view. They believe that if their decisions and actions eventually foul the atmosphere, pollute the land and water, or bring disease or war to the people, it doesn't matter. They will have taken their profit, or gained their fame, and will be dead and won't have to deal with it. Those decisions and actions would probably be vastly different, and made only after long and careful consideration, if the people making them knew that they would be living on this planet in future lifetimes in whatever environment and social climate they had created.

ADVENTURE UNLIMITED

The mind has no limitations, except for those we are willing to accept. Through our minds, we are free to travel in time and space. There is no limit to how far in the past one may venture with regression. How and when did your soul come into existence? You can explore and remember that instant in the beginnings of time when you first became aware that you had an individual existence. You will remember the creative evolution of man—an unusual insight into why you are here, how you came to be here, and why the evolutionists and the creationists are both right and wrong.

Past life regression opens a door onto the Universe. Through regression you can trace the history of the Universe, this planet, and the history of yourself as an unlimited spirit. You can discover whether there have been highly advanced civilizations in the distant past which have vanished without a physical trace. You can discover whether there has been contact with life from other places in the Universe, or if such stories are fanciful, wishful thinking.

By exploring your origins, and the reason for your existence, you can discover your ultimate destination. You can explore the Great Unknown, death, and come to understand it as the normal and desirable end of a cycle of learning in the physical world which opens the door on our more natural existence in the non-physical world. You will come to see this world as a sort of boarding school where we come for varying school terms, at the end of which we return home to the non-physical world for vacation, evaluation and work on the next plan.

THE PRACTICAL ASPECTS

While there are many exotic and esoteric applications for past life regression, essentially its most important application is in improving the quality of your everyday life.

You can use these psychologically sound techniques to explore your past experiences to understand how they have shaped your present life, and yourself. You will learn to like, love and be tolerant of yourself, which are the first steps in being able to like, love and be tolerant of others. You will gain insight into the reasons for the particular relationships you have with the people around you, and uncover information which will help improve those relationships. You will gain understanding of why you fear certain situations, people or things, and be able to rid yourself of those fears. You will remember information which will help you in your chosen careers. You will gain insight into developing strong, fulfilling marriages, and find solid, useful information which will make child rearing easier.

Past life regression is a marvelous tool to help you to reshape your present self and your present life, and provide you with great adventure at the same time.

Pull up your couch or chair and get ready to travel to the far corners of the world, and the far reaches of time. Tuck a hankie in your pocket. There may be tears of laughter, and sorrow. You may find lives of compassion or cruelty, generosity or selfishness, courage or cowardice, love or hate.

Whatever you find, enjoy your adventure and put the information to constructive use. Remember that what you did in those lifetimes are the actions which shaped your present life. The things you do today will affect your tomorrows.

Happy travels!

STAY IN TOUCH

On the following pages you will find some of the books now available on related subjects. Your book dealer stocks most of these and will stock new titles in the Llewellyn series as they become available. We urge your patronage.

To obtain our full catalog write for our bimonthly news magazine/catalog, *Llewellyn's New Worlds of Mind and Spirit.* A sample copy is free, and it will continue coming to you at no cost as long as you are an active mail customer. Or you may subscribe for just $10.00 in the U.S.A. and Canada ($20.00 overseas, first class mail). Many bookstores also have *New Worlds* available to their customers. Ask for it.

Llewellyn's New Worlds of Mind and Spirit
P.O. Box 64383-359, St. Paul, MN 55164-0383, U.S.A.

TO ORDER BOOKS AND TAPES

If your book dealer does not have the books described, you may order them directly from the publisher by sending full price in U.S. funds, plus $3.00 for postage and handling for orders *under* $10.00; $4.00 for orders *over* $10.00. There are no postage and handling charges for orders over $50.00. Postage and handling rates are subject to change. We ship UPS whenever possible. Delivery guaranteed. Provide your street address as UPS does not deliver to P.O. Boxes. UPS to Canada requires a $50.00 minimum order. Allow 4-6 weeks for delivery. Orders outside the U.S.A. and Canada: Airmail—add retail price of book; add $5.00 for each non-book item (tapes, etc.); add $1.00 per item for surface mail. Mail orders to:

LLEWELLYN PUBLICATIONS
P.O. Box 64383-359, St. Paul, MN 55164-0383, U.S.A.

HOW TO MEET & WORK WITH SPIRIT GUIDES
by Ted Andrews

We often experience spirit contact in our lives but fail to recognize it for what it is. Now you can learn to access and attune to beings such as guardian angels, nature spirits and elementals, spirit totems, archangels, gods and goddesses—as well as family and friends after their physical death.

Contact with higher soul energies strengthens the will and enlightens the mind. Through a series of simple exercises, you can safely and gradually increase your awareness of spirits and your ability to identify them. You will learn to develop an intentional and directed contact with any number of spirit beings. Discover meditations to open up your subconscious. Learn which acupressure points effectively stimulate your intuitive faculties. Find out how to form a group for spirit work, use crystal balls, perform automatic writing, attune your aura for spirit contact, use sigils to contact the great archangels and much more! Read *How to Meet and Work with Spirit Guides* and take your first steps through the corridors of life beyond the physical.

0–87542–008–7, 192 pgs., mass market, illus.   **$4.99**

HOW TO UNCOVER YOUR PAST LIVES
by Ted Andrews

Knowledge of your past lives can be extremely reward-ing. It can assist you in opening to new depths within your own psychological makeup. It can provide greater insight into present circumstances with loved ones, career and health. It is also a lot of fun.

Now Ted Andrews shares with you nine different tech-niques that you can use to access your past lives. Between techniques, Andrews discusses issues such as karma and how it is expressed in your present life; the source of past life information; soul mates and twin souls; proving past lives; the mysteries of birth and death; animals and rein-carnation; abortion and pre-mature death; and the role of reincarnation in Christianity.

To explore your past lives, you need only use one or more of the techniques offered. Complete instructions are provided for a safe and easy regression. Learn to dowse to pinpoint the years and places of your lives with great accuracy, make your own self-hypnosis tape, attune to the incoming child during pregnancy, use the tarot and the cabala in past life meditations, keep a past life journal and more.

0-87542-022-2, 240 pgs., mass market, illus. **$3.95**

HOW TO SEE AND READ THE AURA
by Ted Andrews

Everyone has an aura—the three-dimensional, shape-and-color-changing energy field that surrounds all matter. And anyone can learn to see and experience the aura more effectively. There is nothing magical about the process. It simply involves a little understanding, time, practice and perseverance.

Do some people make you feel drained? Do you find some rooms more comfortable and enjoyable to be in? Have you ever been able to sense the presence of other people before you actually heard or saw them? If so, you have experienced another person's aura. In this practical, easy-to-read manual, you receive a variety of exercises to practice alone and with partners to build your skills in aura reading and interpretation. Also, you will learn to balance your aura each day to keep it vibrant and strong so others cannot drain your vital force.

Learning to see the aura not only breaks down old barriers—it also increases sensitivity. As we develop the ability to see and feel the more subtle aspects of life, our intuition unfolds and increases, and the childlike joy and wonder of life returns.

0-87542-013-3, 160 pgs., mass market, illus.   **$3.95**

A PRACTICAL GUIDE TO PAST LIFE REGRESSION
by Florence Wagner McClain

Have you ever felt that there had to be more to life than this? Have you ever met someone and felt an immediate kinship? Have you ever visited a strange place and felt that you had been there before? Have you struggled with frustrations and fears which seem to have no basis in your present life? Are you afraid of death? Have you ever been curious about reincarnation or maybe just interested enough to be skeptical?

This book presents a simple technique that you can use to obtain past life information *today*. There are no mysterious preparations, no groups to join, no philosophy to which you must adhere. You don't even have to believe in reincarnation. The tools are provided for you to make your own investigations, find your own answers and make your own judgements as to the validity of the information and its usefulness to you.

Whether you believe in reincarnation or not, past life regression remains a powerful and valid tool for self-exploration. Information procured through this procedure can be invaluable for personal growth and inner healing, no matter what its source. Florence McClain's guidebook is an eminently sane and capable guide for those who wish to explore their possible past lives or conduct regressions themselves.

0-87542-510-0, 160 pgs., 5¼ x 8, softcover $7.95

**THE LLEWELLYN PRACTICAL GUIDE TO THE
DEVELOPMENT OF PSYCHIC POWERS**
by Denning & Phillips
You may not realize it, but you already have the ability to
use ESP, Astral Vision and Clairvoyance, Divination,
Dowsing, Prophecy, and Communication with Spirits.

Written by two of the most knowledgeable experts in the
world of psychic development, this book is a complete
course—teaching you, step-by-step, how to develop
these powers that actually have been yours since birth.
Using the techniques, you will soon be able to move
objects at a distance, see into the future, know the
thoughts and feelings of another person, find lost objects
and locate water using your no-longer latent talents.

Psychic powers are as much a natural ability as any other
talent. You'll learn to play with these new skills, working
with groups of friends to accomplish things you never
would have believed possible before reading this book.
The text shows you how to make the equipment you can
use, the exercises you can do—many of them at any time,
anywhere—and how to use your abilities to change your
life and the lives of those close to you. Many of the exercises are presented in forms that can be adapted as games
for pleasure and fun, as well as development.
0-87542-191-1, 272 pgs., 5¼ x 8, illus., softcover $8.95

DOORS TO OTHER WORLDS
A Practical Guide to Communicating with Spirits
by Raymond Buckland

There has been a revival of spiritualism in recent years, with more and more people attempting to communicate with disembodied spirits via talking boards, séances, and all forms of mediumship (e.g., allowing another spirit to make use of your vocal chords, hand muscles, etc., while you remain in control of your body). The movement, which began in 1848 with the Fox sisters of New York, has attracted the likes of Abraham Lincoln and Queen Victoria, and even blossomed into a full-scale religion with regular services of hymns, prayers, Bible-reading and sermons along with spirit communication.

Doors to Other Worlds is for *anyone* who wishes to communicate with spirits, as well as for the less adventurous who simply wish to satisfy their curiosity about the subject. Explore the nature of the Spiritual Body, learn how to prepare yourself to become a medium, experience for yourself the trance state, clairvoyance, psychometry, table tipping and levitation, talking boards, automatic writing, spiritual photography, spiritual healing, distant healing, channeling, development circles, and also learn how to avoid spiritual fraud.

0-87542-061-3, 272 pgs., 5¼ x 8, illus., softcover $10.00